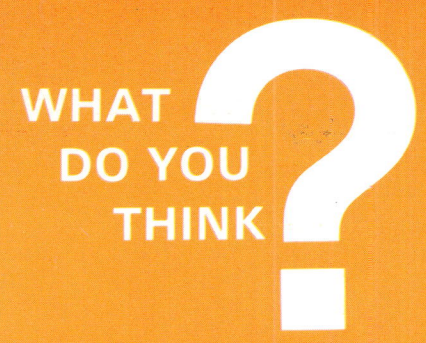

WHAT DO YOU THINK ?

*Tick off the **best** answer in each section — and check your answers.*

1. Why do we need to pray as a family?
A   To help us live better lives.
B   To get to heaven.
C   To come closer to each other.
D   To come closer to God.

2. What's the best method of family prayer?
A   The Rosary and prayers we have learnt by heart.
B   Applying a passage of scripture to ourselves and praying about it.
C   A chat about our lives together and prayers based on questions.
D   All of these approaches.

3. What is absolutely essential to our family prayers?
A   A good, sound Family Prayer book.
B   A lot of love in the family.
C   A strong link between our family prayer and the Mass.
D   The Bible.

4. Which of the following words best sums up family prayer as it should be?
A   enjoyable.
B   reverent.
C   natural.
D   a duty.

ANSWERS

1. C. —Our closeness as a "domestic church" is Our Father's greatest desire for us; it is the way towards closeness to God and the best way of bringing the good news to others.

2. D.—Our approach should depend on the ages of the children and on our own experiences and **growth** in prayer as a family. But we should take a good look at our prayer if there is one of these approaches that we never use.

3. C.—A good prayer book and a Bible are good helps to Family Prayer but a link with the Eucharist is **essential.** Even though we fail to love each other during the day, we come to prayer, as to the Mass, to ask forgiveness, to praise and appreciate each other, to listen, to thank, to decide once again to offer ourselves. All these elements of the Mass should be part of our family life, of our prayer and of our preparation for Sunday Mass (see page 25).

4. A.—Family Prayer will not always come naturally, especially when we are getting used to something different — as will happen at times if we are growing in our prayers. It is obviously a duty, of course, and should be a time of real reverence, (for each other as well as for God), but there is something seriously wrong with our prayer if it is not a time when we regularly experience closeness and enjoyment as a family.

1

excuses

I HAVE NO TIME

People today live under a great many pressures. We are constantly working to deadlines, and all kinds of demands are being made on our time and attention. Often enough, we are so busy that we don't even get a chance to sit down and plan and decide what we most want for our children. But the simple fact is that our children cannot and will not learn to pray unless they learn it from us, their parents. If they do not see and hear adults praying they will get the impression that prayer is kid's stuff.

AW, MAMMY, WAIT TILL THIS PROGRAMME IS OVER!

A recent survey showed that the greatest obstacle to family prayer is television. Daddy wants to see the news and somebody's favourite programme comes immediately after that. It is easy to see how a child could begin to see family prayer as a boring time — taking him away from something enjoyable. So it would seem to be important to get together and work out a fixed time that would be suitable for everyone — and to stick to it.

BUT PEOPLE MIGHT COME IN . . .

Would you like to think that a family didn't pray because **you** dropped in? Wouldn't you be far more impressed with the family that asked you to join them? Our parents weren't embarrassed to do that. So if friends or neighbours do call during your prayer-time, that needn't disrupt the prayers — you can be an example and inspiration to them and an influence for good.

I'LL SAY MY OWN PRAYERS!

No one can deny the importance of private prayers. But what chance is there for our family life if we don't even pray together as a family? The child who wants to opt out is probably just testing us and as parents we need to insist. Of course, we can only insist up to a certain point with our teenagers — perhaps it is best to include them in our petitions rather than have a running fight. But it is as important for them as it is for the younger children to know that their parents pray — and to **see** them praying.

PRAYER IS A BORE!

Yes, sometimes prayer is boring — sometimes listening to each other is boring too! That's not a good reason for giving up family prayer, however — that's acting on our feelings. But obviously there are certain things we can do to make prayer time more attractive. That's the purpose of this booklet . . .

WHERE TO PRAY

The kitchen, the couch in the sitting-room, around the dining-room table, in bed, in the car. Each family knows what suits them best and what helps them most to concentrate. Many families find they can pray well in the car — or around the table after a meal may be the best place for a family that is scattering immediately afterwards.

At the table The table, in fact, is often compared to the altar in the Church and it is one of the few places where we can all be together as a family. In teenage families, the table may be the only place where they can all have a few minutes of prayer — after the evening meal is over and before some of them leave for meetings, clubs, etc.

In the bedroom For younger families, the bedroom is hard to beat as a place for prayer — just before the children are settled for the night. At any other time of the day it is a choice between prayer and something more attractive, like a game or a television programme. Now it's a straight choice between sleep and holding onto Mammy and Daddy for a few minutes more. Children are at their most receptive at this time of the day and many parents find that even their quietest child is liable to ask all kinds of questions and talk about friends, school, fears, successes and worries as the parents sit on the bed. Prayer at this time can be a very pleasant experience — particularly when we have the time and energy for a bedtime chat at the same time.

Choosing the right time and place, as we have just seen, is obviously very important to the success of our family prayer — as far as possible, we need to make it a special time together rather than a dull boring interlude that has no effect on the rest of the day.

CHANGING THE SCENERY Some families find it helps to vary things a bit — to kneel in the dark around a candle placed on a stool in the kitchen, or to go into the sitting-room once a week, sit on the floor around the electric fire and turn off the lights. The children love that — watch how they snuggle closer. Other families kneel before the crucifix or a holy picture, or they bring over a statue to make the occasion more special. (See the next article "No Religious Objects Please".)

MUSIC TO MATCH Variety, in fact, is a great help to family prayer, so that it won't just become mechanical. That is why there are different approaches suggested in this booklet. Or one excellent way to vary prayer-time is to introduce singing — children love singing and a hymn can be both enjoyable and meaningful for them, especially if we spend a few minutes beforehand asking what they think the words mean. (Parents themselves, of course, don't have to know what the words mean — the children can often tell them.) It is not difficult to find an inexpensive little hymn-book with a good selection of hymns — like *Alleluia Amen* or the *Veritas Hymnal*.

TO KNEEL OR NOT TO KNEEL
Recently, many families have begun to sit for prayers, which would have been unthinkable a generation ago. Sitting has the advantage of drawing the family closer together — some Daddies have been known to support four children on their knees while praying! — but there is also a lot to be said for kneeling, at least occasionally, to let the children see prayer time as something quite special.

BISCUITS AT BEDTIME Another little help is to associate prayer-time with something quite pleasant — like ending with a cup of drinking chocolate or a biscuit. The children go off to sleep with an extra glow — they know they're special to us, and there's a deeper bond between the whole family.

HELPS TO PRAYER

I never was one of your 'holy' Catholics. The opposite in fact. A sensible modern Mrs. and proud of it.

Growing up I was often put off by those Holy Pictures on the walls of our home that looked at you into every corner of the room. They were so gloomy and strange and sad and unreal. Then there was the nightly ritual of the Rosary with its groans for the Hails and the Holys. Mentally I was making notes that I would be 'sensible' about things like this when I got older.

So when Joe and I set up home, we certainly didn't clutter the place with religious objects. We gave away the Sacred Heart picture that someone embarrassed me with when we got married. None of that for us. Nor gaudy statues. We hung the Rosary beads on a hook in the wardrobe and never got around to using them. No holy pictures either. Very little evidence, in fact, that we were Catholics. I would go to Mass alright but I wasn't going to be identified with that lot. Instead of pictures, I put up posters that told me what love is and

No Religious Objects Please!

by Mary O'Sullivan

reminded me to be patient and gentle and spoke about friendship. Good sensible mind-raising stuff and 'nice' principles. Nothing Christian about them, mind you, but weren't we all human anyway . . .

I WAS FLABBERGASTED

Then I did a Parish Renewal Weekend and I was flabbergasted. For the first time I realised that I was throwing out the baby with the bath water. Okay — I didn't like gaudy pictures, but what was I handing on to my children? What chance had they of keeping the faith if they saw no evidence of it even on the walls of our home. Vatican II, I was told, said that we were a little church in our own home, but our little church (if it was one) had lost its heart. Not that holy pictures on the walls would have proved anything. But their absence spoke volumes.

So one of the first changes I made when I came home from Parish Renewal was to buy a statue of our Lady (that I liked) and put it in the window. I got a crucifix for the hall and a few cheap pictures for the bedrooms. It was nice, you know — it suddenly made the place more of a home. I had been so busy reacting against the home I had been brought up in that I had forgotten so many of the things I had loved about it.

I WAS BACK TO SQUARE ONE

I find, though, that it's easy to make a big change, and then two weeks later I'm back to square one. It was Joe pointed out to me, that the changes might as well never have happened. You see, even after I had changed things around a bit, I would never stop to look at the pictures or objects; I never talked to the children about them. They were more ornaments than religious objects.

Now the statue of Our Lady is on the fridge and it is taken down to the table for the evening prayers; the crucifix is on the wall of the dining-room and we kneel around it whenever we say a decade of the Rosary; the pictures are on the walls beside the children's beds and we use them occasionally in our chats with the children. And I'm beginning to understand that bit about a family being a little Church.

The standard of religious objects and pictures has been improving in recent years with a distinct move away from the 'sugary' portrayal of Jesus, Mary and the Saints. Try to ensure that you have an attractive religious picture or object in each room, especially in the main living areas and the children's

bedrooms. Somewhere in the house there should be a crucifix, a simple picture of our Holy Father — and also some photos of family members on their big Church occasions like Matrimony, Baptism, First Communion, etc.

There is no single right way to pray, but keep a few good principles in mind.

Firstly, there is a lot to be said for our traditional prayers. They have stood the test of time and have come to us as part of the richness passed down from generation to generation. We should not discard them lightly. The Rosary, for example, is a beautiful family prayer — some families like to talk about a single mystery each night before saying that decade.

There is always, of course, the danger that familiar prayers will become routine. So a little chat about the meaning of a prayer or about the day's events can be an excellent way of starting our prayer and keeping it fresh and meaningful.

How to pray

Reading and reflecting on scripture is another aspect of prayer we should not neglect and which tends to becom more important as our children enter their teens. A natural way to introduc it is to make the Sunday Gospel part of our family prayer, or to use a helpful little prayerbook (like ''Famil Prayers'' by Peter Byrne, C.Ss.R.) tha contains reflections on scripture.

Prayer-time, or course, should be a time of reflection — not just on God and scripture but on our own family life and on how we treat each other. And questions are one of the best wa of getting us to stop and think and to draw closer as a family unit. There is now growing emphasis on prayer that is based on such questions.

We present here the experience of a few families. They are not perfect models, but they are trying in their own way to make their prayer meaningful

praying together with the children

When Veronica was making her first Holy Communion, we were invited to the school for a series of three talks. They were very good, for they helped us to realise that we were neglecting prayer with our children.

We'll give it a try

One of the most interesting things that the teacher suggested was that we should come together at the childrens' bedtime, and each of the family give one instance of where we showed love to someone that day and one instance of where we didn't love, and we should ask forgiveness of the one we offended. I don't know what possessed us to try it for, as far as we can make out, none of the other parents did. It turned out to be one of the best things that has ever happened to us as a family.

It looks like a flop.

We started the next night. Joe (my husband said he had smiled at a lot of people that day and he thanked God for that goodness in him. At first I couldn't think of anything good I had done but I mumbled something about making coffee for Joe. Would the children like to tell us when they had shown love? — No. Not a word! So on we went. Joe said he had been impatient with me that morning and had shouted at me. He said he was sorry and he kissed me. Not the kind of prayers I was used to, but I began to see the point! I said I had been grumbling and in bad form with everyone all day and I was sorry now and I asked each one to forgive me. Now the children's turn. Nothing! Did they think we were queer? We coaxed them, but nothing. So we all said an Act of Contrition — and I noticed that Mark and Carmel didn't know the words!

And so the next night. And the next night. Not a word from the children. We wondered if it was such a good idea then. It wasn't working for us. Until Veronica came in, after about two weeks, strong on her good points, not so open about her weaknessses. But she was talking, and from there on the other children gradually came in. And that has completely changed our family life. The children see us now as human, not faultless, needing their forgiveness. They know they can come to us now and admit their failings. Even 'serious' things have tumbled out in those end-of-day sessions — like stealing or lies — and all kinds of things have cropped up that we might never have known about each other. We have had some terrific moments together as a family — like the night when I said I showed love when I made vegetable soup for the children and Mark said how he had shown love when he ate it even though he didn't like it.

Thank God we tried

We also see this as a powerful indirect way of teaching morality—our children now know what it means to love and not to love. And we are not just looking at our faults (as when I was a child) but at our goodness too, and admitting to each other that God's great goodness is working in us all and drawing us together in love.

OUR PRAYERS AT HOME

by John McIntyre

I don't like our family prayers to be too stereo-typed or formal. For that reason we do not have any rigidly set pattern of prayer. I'll tell you what we normally do first and then I'll tell you how we vary it.

SET PRAYER

We use the prayers that the children are learning in school. Early on in primary school, they learned to sign a Morning Prayer and an Evening Prayer. They like to sing these prayers so we encourage them by joining in with them — initially, I felt a bit silly, but I take singing with the children in my stride now.

Morning: O my God, you love me: you're with me night and day. I want to love you always in in all I do and say. I'll try to please you, Father. Bless me through the day. Amen.

Evening: God our Father, I come to say thank you for your love today. Thank you for my family and all the friends you give to me. Guard me in the dark of night and in the morning send your light. Amen.

We also say a few traditional prayers — the Our Father, the Hail Mary and the Morning Offering in the morning around the table; the act of Contrition and also the prayer to Saint Francis at night (around the table after tea, as our eldest is so often going out to Scouts or football).

PRAYERS FROM QUESTIONS:

In addition to these set prayers, we try various things to make sure that prayer will not just be words rhymed off. Sometimes we ask: 'What do we need to thank God for today?" and we usually get a list of vegetables, relatives, animals, house-hold objects, machines, teachers — especially from our youngest who, in her simplicity, knows more about prayer than we do. Other questions we ask on different occasions are, "What (and who) do we need to pray for?" "What has someone in the family done recently that I would like to thank God for?" "What do we need to say we are sorry for?" That last one is more difficult but I think it is very important for us to be able to say we are sorry to one another for the way we hurt each other.

11

SAINTS ON FRIDAYS

We also have three special nights — Friday, Saturday and Sunday.

On Friday, we let the children stay up an extra half-hour because they don't have to go to school the next day. At bedtime, instead of the usual prayers, Rosemary and I read them a story from the Children's Bible or the lives of the Saints (Alice Curtayne's "Irish Saints for Boys and Girls" is excellent, and we also have a big three-volume "Story Library of the Saints" published by Harwin Press which the children love). We don't say any formal prayers with our children on Friday night, but I see all this as a vital part of our Family Prayers as we introduce our children to the Saints.

PLANS FROM THE GOSPEL

On Saturday, we prepare for Mass by reading the Sunday Gospel. Then, starting with the parents, we each say what strikes us about the passage and we try to apply it to our daily lives and our plans for the coming week. Whenever that leaves us blank, we take a little bit of one of the prayers of the Mass and apply it in the same way. This can change mere words like: "Heaven and earth are full of your glory" into an awareness of the glory of God in nature and in people all around us — and it helps

Some 'starter' questions that can be used to make the family prayer more real:

us to look at the practical ways in which we can glorify God ourselves. The value of this exercise is that the children are beginning to appreciate the importance of the Bible here and now in their everyday lives, and it also helps them to link prayer at home with prayer in the Church.

SUNDAY MISCELLANY

On Sunday, we replace prayer with a chat at bedtime — usually two chats as there are two different bedtimes in our house. Rosemary and I tell the children: "Ask us any questions you like" and we answer as best we can, although we often have to tell them that we do not know the answers. Some of the questions we've been asked recently include: "What is heaven like?" "Why did the Jews hate Jesus?" "Who was Moses' Mammy and Daddy?" and "What's the worst sin in the world?" (We said, it was not loving — being indifferent. What do you think?) They ask us about death and angels and babies and priests and Mass and rules and saints and away beyond religion to questions about us and our childhood and animals and gardening and grandparents and cooking and the presents they want for next Christmas. Then we say a short little prayer before putting out the light. Ask them their favourite time in the week and it is always Sunday night.

(1) What are you going to do to love others today? Smile? Say hello? Wash dishes? Bring in coal? Come when you're called? Be cheerful?

(2) What do you want to thank God for today?

(3) Who do you need to pray for? Relatives? Missionaries? Sick people? Our Pope? Someone in the family?

(4) What are you anxious about that you would like to ask everyone to pray for?

(5) Choose one person in the family at a time and everyone can say what this person did today that you would like to thank God for.

(6) Tell one time when you were hurt by someone in this family today — and forgive that person.

(7) Tell one time when you showed love today and thank God for that.

(8) Tell one time you didn't show love today and ask for forgiveness of the one you offended.

At home with the Rosary

It can be all too easy to opt for a very super-ficial, baby-type family prayer that leaves out the heart and centre of our Catholic faith — like "God bless Mammy and Daddy and Kevin and Mary and Auntie May and bring us all up safe to heaven when we die." Parents in their goodness can be so anxious to get down to the level of faith of their youngest that the children never experience the real prayer and faith of adults. How else can they learn to pray?

We should think well before we abandon the Rosary, the prayer which ensures that we regu-larly spend some time thinking of the central mysteries of our faith. Far from being out-of-date, it is more needed today than in the past and is the favourite prayer of many deeply spiri-tual people in the Church — including our Holy Father. And it strengthens our devotion to our Mother Mary.

If, however, our children see the Rosary as boring, perhaps that is a sign that we need to spend a little time preparing, teaching, talking, asking questions . . . Better to say a decade a day that is meaningful than a full Rosary that is merely mechanical.

Together on a Sunday

by Gerry and Pat Quinn

Praying on beads (or on knots on a string) goes away back to pre-Christian times. The custom was adopted by monks in the Eastern Church in the third century and gradually spread West. By the 10th century, the Rosary was firmly established in Ireland. In England, it was known as the Paternoster and Paternoster Row became famous because of the craftsmen there who produced strings of Rosary beads. Down through the centuries the power of the Rosary has been stressed by many great saints, notably St. Dominic and St. Francis de Sales. In our own day, its importance has been highlighted by the miracles at Lourdes and Fatima and by the work of Fr. Peyton who promoted the Rosary as a family prayer. Alternatives to the Rosary beads are the Paidrín beag, (the traditional 'little beads' — a single decade in circular form) or the Rosary ring — a ring with a cross and ten little teeth for counting the Aves.

We say the Rosary as a family every Sunday. Sometimes we say it sitting around the table after our evening meal; most times we turn off the television in the living-room and say it there. If we have been away to Granny's at the week-end we say the Rosary in the car on the way home.

There are six of us, so two of us have to share a decade — usually the two little ones. (They wouldn't forego their turn at giving out their part for anything; they'd feel left out.) The person giving out a decade always mentions a special intention before starting. Tonight, for example, I offered my decade for a couple whose marriage is in trouble.

WE TALK ABOUT THE DECADE

We take a little longer about saying the Rosary than when I was a child — of course, we were saying the Rosary every evening then and it was a chore to be dashed through in as many minutes under ten as possible. Now that we're saying it once a week, we're more relaxed and informal about it all. We don't kneel. And instead of just announcing the name of the mystery at the beginning of a decade, we stop and talk about it — and that makes all the difference. Tonight at the Visitation we talked about Elizabeth being Mary's cousin, how Elizabeth had a baby in her tummy as well as Mary and how the baby leaped for joy when Mary greeted Elizabeth. We talked about how a new calendar had begun from the time of Christ's birth — and our son Joseph asked how long Jesus had been preaching "before he got on the Cross". So we just talk about each mystery and, when we're ready, we say the decade.

DRAWING US TOGETHER

We know the children like saying the Rosary. You know when children like something and when they hate something — they have a million ways of letting you know. John, our twelve-year-old, says it's the only time in the week when he feels close to the rest of the family. That it's the time when any anger and annoyance he has with us tends to melt away. This all makes the Rosary a very special time when we sit around together and talk. It is a time of closeness and forgiveness. Tonight I mentioned how much it had meant to me yesterday that Cormac had noticed how tired I was and had brought me down a pillow — that the Visitation was still going on! Our ten-year-old daughter, too, often finds that she can tell us all during Rosary time how she feels about things that are annoying or worrying her. There is a sense, in fact, of togetherness and of us all doing something important together.

I'm sure it is something that the children will remember when they grow older, something they will talk about and remember long after they have left our home.

Family Mealtimes

by **Fiona Perrem**

I'm one to be writing about family meals! There are times when a visitor comes in for tea and the children act up and the table is a mess and I feel so embarrassed that I'd rather eat *underneath* the table. Anyway, at the moment, we're trying to change our evening meal from an "eat-and-run" session to a real family meal.

It's a constant fight

In our house it is a constant fight to try and get everyone together at mealtimes. Melanie (7) wants to "finish watching this programme". Killian (10) is grumbling that he needs to eat fast and clear off with his friends. Damian (1½) is screaming and needs to be fed *now*. Well, why would you wait another half-hour putting up with that racket? Peter has a chance of doing some overtime and we can do with the money. Or he comes in jaded and he wants to sit with a newspaper "to unwind". But I talked to Peter and the children and I said surely as a family there's something wrong if we can't have one half-hour or so in the day together. And they sort of agreed . . . .

Helping us to slow down

We start the meal with grace. I like the

old prayer we've always had — apart from the word "bounty" — **"Bless us, O Lord, and these your gifts which of your goodness we are about to receive through Christ Our Lord, Amen"**. Some days, we ask everyone at the table to say a short prayer, even if that means that the dinner ends up a bit cooler. I encourage them to pray for each other as well as the neighbours and relatives — and the poor who have no food. Sometimes their prayers are very simple and touching. Peter often prays for us to "listen to each other". I need to be reminded of that! Other times, they want to sing the grace that they have learnt in school:

Bless us O God, as we sit together.
Bless the food we eat today
Bless the hands that made the food.
Bless us O God. Amen.

Other times they just show off — especially in front of a visitor — and I cringe. Or one of them is sulking and "won't pray". But I really believe that prayer at the beginning of a meal is full of grace — it stops us in our tracks, pulls us away from all the busy-ness and helps us to slow down.

It's easier to ignore the children

I would love mealtime to be an enjoyable time, a listening time, a fun time. But so often, things have happened during the day that I want to talk to Peter about and I haven't had a good chat with him since he came home. It's easier to ignore the children — except to nag at them for slabbering or arguing or interrupting. It can even be hard enough, too, to get them started at times. Peter and I try to set the pace by saying a few things (briefly!) about our day and then we get them talking about their day. Or we pick a good question like "What are you most afraid of?" or "What would you like for your next birthday?" and ask everyone to take turns in answering it. It can even be a real eye-opener to ask: "What was the best/worst thing that happened to each of you today?" It's difficult at times, of course, but I must say I've got to know our children and Peter much better, thanks to slowing down and listening and encouraging that mealtime conversation.

We're like the nine lepers

Mostly we're like the nine lepers. We forget to thank God — or anyone else — for our meals. But thanks to our children we have begun to sing the little grace after meals that they learned at school:

Thank you, God, for the food we have
eaten
Thank you, God, for all our friends
Thank you, God, for everything
Thank you, God, Amen.

It's a queer state of affairs when the children start teaching the parents to pray!

Here's a simple 'Grace before Meals' that children love to sing — it's to the tune of Edelweiss and links up the family meal with the Sunday Eucharist. For there is no better way to make the Mass meaningful than to learn to forgive, to listen, to thank and appreciate around our own family table — all these elements are important parts of our celebration as a parish family around the altar on Sundays.

BLESS OUR FAMILY, BLESS THIS FOOD
YOU HAVE CHOSEN TO GIVE US,
BLESS THE HANDS THAT MADE THIS MEAL
AND EARNED THE MONEY TO FEED US.
HELP US ASK QUESTIONS AND LISTEN AND LAUGH
AND THANK AND FORGIVE AT THIS TABLE
SO THAT WE MAY GO PREPARED
ON SUNDAY TO JOIN WITH YOUR PEOPLE

Trip to Confession

by Mary O'Sullivan

It was a last minute rush

We were one of those families that had drifted miles from regular Confession. Every five, six, seven months, guilt would get the better of us and I would scold Veronica and Mark for "neglecting the Sacraments", and Joe or myself would take them off. It was usually a last-minute rush, scattered, quite unpleasant and very far from being a family occasion.

Chips and change

As a result of our Parish Renewal Weekend, we decided to go to Confession as a family once a month — the last Saturday in the month, in fact, so that we wouldn't forget. Also to make it a family affair and to celebrate on the way home with a few bags of chips. Here's how we go about it.

Telling the children our 'sins'

Before we go, we sit down together as a family and talk about what we are going to do. We start with a prayer to Our Lady to pray with us for the graces of the Sacrament of Reconciliation. Then we tell the children the main areas that we are going to confess — not going through the Ten Commandments or anything, but looking at the people we live with — family and neighbours and the people at work or at school. My main sins are with Joe and the children (nagging, not listening, criticising), then there's the gossip about

my neighbours and my neglect of the ones that need me most.

Not rhyming off a list

Joe or myself always begins and then the children chip in, clarifying for themselves what they will confess. Not that we're putting them under any pressure to tell us specific sins, of course — but I'm convinced that this all helps them (and myself) to prepare more fully and to become aware of the areas in our lives where we need to change. It certainly gets away from the old rhyming-off of a list of "sins".

Final preparations

At this stage we usually ask forgiveness of each other for what we have just talked about with each other. Then we talk about how we are going to try to treat each other differently. Or I find myself at times giving a little talk on the need to be really sorry or the need to thank God afterwards. (Preaching, maybe, is one of my sins! But I don't think a bit of a sermon does any harm now and again — I wish more parents bothered.)

We go as a family

We make a point of trying to go together as a family to Confession (which isn't always possible) — and, of course, on the way home we get out bags of chips. Mark, mind you, is so fond of chips that there's absolutely no danger of forgetting our monthly outing of Reconciliation . . . .

The story of Zacchaeus is used to introduce school children to confession.

Couple prayer

We parents are the most important part of family prayer. Our lives, our love for one another, our faith, our prayer together, our patience, our listening, the way we deal with a crisis — are the greatest lessons our children will ever learn. Without our living faith, family prayer is no more than window dressing. So we must not be afraid to expose our children to that prayer and that faith.

Remember your own parents. You may often have been bored at prayertime but, as they prayed, you only had to look at their faces to know they believed very deeply.

Now, in order to keep that prayer really vital, we need to be growing in our own faith and specifically in our own vocation to be a couple. We are the sacramental centre of our own little "domestic Church". We need to pray together. God has called us to be two in one, not to come to him separately. And the main thrust of our prayer should be to love one another more, to forgive and appreciate one another, to remove whatever is preventing me from being in love with you, my husband, my wife.

An important part of that prayer, then, is to ask each other questions like: "How have I hurt you recently?" "In what ways would you like me to help you?" After all, there is no point in saying to God: "Do with me what Thou wilt" if we cannot say it to each other. That chat together can be a tremendous opener to prayer . . . .

Married prayer

by Pat and Mary Cunningham

For a long time we saw prayer as some kind of obligation, very much on a one to one basis between each of us and God. The fact that we were married didn't make very much difference to our prayers.

Whenever we had disagreements — over money, children, sex, in-laws, etc. — we always believed that we were better to face them rather than smooth over them in the hope that they would work out. We saw the value in keeping on talking and listening in these little conflicts. As we talked, however, it often struck us that we should pray to God to help us through these tensions and bring us closer together. That was the beginning of our "married prayer".

At first this prayer together was very general rather than for any specific need, but then we began to realise that praying "to be more loving" wasn't really very helpful. We had such different ideas about how to spend money that when the topic came up we really needed the grace to *listen* to each other. So we began to pray for more specific graces like this.

Moreover, if I pray for a grace like being cheerful with Mary in the mornings, a private prayer may not make much difference. When we pray together, however, that puts me under a certain pressure to cheer up, to change. Praying together makes all the difference.

Five minutes on our own

by Hugh and Anna Donnelly

Together with the New Testament We both work at home, so we pray together most mornings for a little while after the children have gone out to work or to school. Normally we sit down and one of us reads a short verse or two from the New Testament. We then have a little discussion on how this applies to us and to our children, and how we can respond to the call that comes in those words. This short reading reminds us of who we are and gives us a sense of direction for that day.

Together before the Sacred Heart After this, we kneel before the Sacred Heart picture and put ourselves and our family under the guidance of the Sacred Heart for the day. We also dedicate our family to the Immaculate Heart of Mary and ask her to guard over us and those we love this day. We thank God for all He has done for us and we lift up to God all those people we resent or dislike and ask Him to bless them and change our hearts. We mention our faults with each other and pray for healing for these. Finally, we say the Lord's Prayer, a Hail Mary, a Glory be to the Father and a prayer asking God to use us in whatever way He wants that day to build up His Church.

Together at night At night-time we pray at our bedside for all our own brothers and sisters and parents and for the whole Church generally, and we often talk in bed for a while and say a short prayer together.

There is no such thing as private prayer

by Fr. Johnny Doherty, C.Ss.R.

A few years ago, a man who was coming to the end of a life-sentence for murder got very frightened. He had become so used to imprisonment over the course of thirty years that the thought of freedom scared him and he applied to the courts for permission to stay on in prison for the rest of his life.

A few years ago, through the second Vatican Council, we as a Catholic people were called into the freedom of the children of God. There has been a lot of confusion and fear since, because in so many ways the "imprisonment" we were under seemed much safer and more secure. Changes have been made, new initiatives have been taken and we are being called to live differently from the way we lived with one another in the Church before the Council.

An important part of that difference is in our prayers. There was always a feeling before the Council, that if we said the correct words at the correct times we would be okay; there was more emphasis on keeping rules and on 'don'ts' than on appreciating and loving each other; prayer was often seen as a duty born of fear and reverence rather than a time of closeness and reconciliation within a family; prayer, too, tended to be rigid and even boring rather than something that changed and grew as a family also changed and grew.

But why all the changes?

It is not easy to now change old habits that are familiar, but it helps to remember why the change is called for. It is because we are asked to become little churches in our own homes. A church, you see, is a community of people rooted in the Eucharist and whose love shines out to others to let them see how Jesus himself loves us. A close family, in other words, makes Jesus real by their very love for one another. That is why, throughout this book, there is so much emphasis on prayer that builds closeness in a family through reconciliation and forgiveness, listening, thanks, offering of ourselves and all the other elements that go to make up our Mass. It is not that on any given evening our prayer has to contain every single one of these elements but we should try to include all of them over a week, as for example, in the plan at the back of this book. And if some of these things seem strange, even foreign to prayer, it is good to be aware that they give meaning to our Sunday Eucharist and help us to live up to our vocation to be little beacons of closeness and love, domestic churches in a world that is darkened by indifference and privacy.

It's private between me and God!

Part of our difficulty, of course, is that many of us have been taught to see prayer as something private between me and God. In fact, there can be no such thing as purely private prayer for us, because we have been called to be a people, a Church, a single Body, and to approach our Father **together**. That is true even when we pray alone. Anytime we choose to pray we need to become aware that prayer is already happening and we are joining in. It is the prayer of our people in Heaven, in Purgatory and throughout the world. It is the prayer of Christ: "that they all may be one, as you, Father, n me, and I in you." So it is obvious that **family** prayer is particularly helpful in teaching us to become aware of others as we join the whole Body of Christ in praying for that unity - which has to begin in the home.

To be pious or passionate?

Our family prayer, then, needs to be a time when we seek to be more one, to be closer to one another. How much more passionate, we may ask, are we becoming as husband and wife with each other? Is our prayer making me as a husband a better listener, more tender towards my wife; is our prayer making me as a wife more sexual with my husband? Or is my prayer just making us more pious? How can we be better in the amount of time we give each other, in appreciation, in real attentiveness? These are the kind of questions we need to take into our prayer. The same is true of us parents with our children. How do each of us need to change so as to listen and be more affectionate and to make time for one another? We need the grace to slow down or to sacrifice some interest in order to be with the rest of the family. Is our prayer having that effect?

A family's greatest sin

Finally, it has become unfashionable to talk about sin but a family's greatest sin is the kind of privacy that is promoted in today's world. Our holiness as a family is our closeness — but it is a closeness and warmth that must touch or neighbours. Part of our prayers, then, is to become aware of the needs of others and to respond to those needs. That's the point of the second half of Jesus' prayer: "that they may be one in us, **so that the world may believe it was you who sent me**".

Prayers of our people

Children ought to grow up knowing these traditional prayers (including the Gloria and Creed from the Mass). The only easy way to learn them, however, is to let the children hear them often enough. It can be a good idea, in fact, to make out a programme to ensure that all of these prayers are said regularly in the home. An odd prize for anyone who can say a given prayer by heart can also be an encouragement to learning them.

Our Father

Our Father, who art in heaven, hallowed by thy name; thy kingdom come, thy will be done on earth as it is in heaven. Give us this day our daily bread; and forgive us our trespasses, as we forgive those who trespass against us; and lead us not into temptation, but deliver us from evil. Amen.

Sign of the Cross

In the name of the Father, and of the Son, and of the Holy Spirit. Amen.

Hail Mary

Hail Mary full of grace, the Lord is with thee; blessed art thou among women, and blessed is the fruit of thy womb, Jesus. Holy Mary, Mother of God, pray for us sinners, now and at the hour of our death, Amen.

Glory be to the Father

Glory be to the Father, and to the Son, and to the Holy Spirit; as it was in the beginning, is now and ever shall be, world without end. Amen.

Prayer to the Holy Spirit

Come, Holy Spirit, fill the hearts of the faithful and kindle in them the fire of your love. Send forth your Spirit, and they shall be created. And you will renew the face of the earth.

O God who has taught the hearts of the faithful by the light of the Holy Spirit, grant us in the same Spirit to be truly wise, and ever to rejoice in his consolation, through Jesus Christ our Lord. Amen.

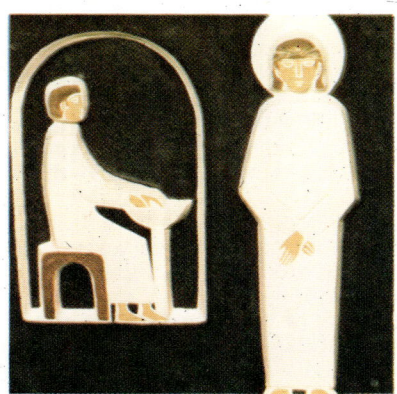

1. Jesus is condemned to death.

2. Jesus receives the cross.

Morning Prayer

O my God, you love me,
you're with me night and day.
I want to love you always
in all I do and say.
I'll try to please you, Father.
Bless me through the day. Amen.

Night Prayer

God, our Father, I come to say
thank you for your love today.
Thank you for my family
and all the friends you give to me.
Guard me in the dark of night
and in the morning send your light.
Amen.

Grace before Meals

Bless us, O God, as we sit together.
Bless the food we eat today.
Bless the hands that made the food.
Bless us, O God. Amen.

Grace after Meals

Thank you, God, for the food
    we have eaten.
Thank you, God, for all our friends.
Thank you, God, for everything.
    Amen.

The Angelus

The Angel of the Lord declared unto
    Mary.
And she conceived of the Holy Spirit.
Hail Mary.....
Behold the handmaid of the Lord.
Be it done unto me according to thy
    word.
Hail Mary.....
And the word was made flesh.
And dwelt among us.
Hail Mary.....
Pray for us O Holy Mother of God,
that we may be made worthy of the
    promises of Christ.

Lord, fill our hearts with your love,
and as you revealed to us by an angel
the coming of your Son as man,
so lead us through his suffering and
death to the glory of his Resurrection,
for he lives and reigns with you and
the Holy Spirit, one God, for ever and
ever. Amen.

Act of Sorrow

O my God, I thank you for loving me.
I am sorry for all my sins, for not
loving others and not loving you. Help
me to live like Jesus and not sin again.
Amen.

3. Jesus falls the first time.

4. Jesus meets his mother.

Acts of Faith

O my God, I believe in you and in all that your holy Church teaches because you have said it and your word is true.

You are the Christ, the Son of the living God. You are my Lord and my God. Lord, I believe, increase my faith.

Act of Hope

O my God, I put my hope in you because I am sure of your promises. Deliver us, Lord, from every evil and grant us peace in our day as we wait in joyful hope for the coming of our Saviour, Jesus Christ.

Act of Charity

O my God, I love you with all my heart, with all my soul, and with all my strength. Lord, increase our love. Help us to love one another.

The Prayer of St. Francis

Lord, make me an instrument of your peace
Where there is hatred let me sow love
Where there is injury, pardon
Where there is discord, union
Where there is doubt, faith
Where there is despair, hope
Where there is darkness, light
Where there is sadness, joy.
Let the aim of my life be to comfort rather than be comforted
To understand rather than be understood
To love rather than be loved.

Prayer of a Husband and Wife

Together, Lord, at the end of the day,
we praise you and we thank you:
For giving us life,
For giving us to one another,
For trusting us with children,
R. Lord, we thank you.

For every experience of love, peace and joy we have had together,
For the successes of our life together,
For the failures which have helped us to know ourselves and each other better.
R. Lord, we thank you.

For the help of our neighbours in time of trouble,
For the needy who compel us to be generous,
R. Lord, we thank you.

For the forgiveness we have received from each other,
For your forgiveness,
R. Lord, we thank you.

5. Simon of Cyrene helps Jesus.

6. Veronica wipes the face of Jesus.

You have taken care of us from the first moment of our life. We know your love will never fail us. With confidence we ask:

That we may be ever faithful,
R. Lord, hear us.

That we may never make light of your gifts,
R. Lord, hear us.

That we may never fail in respect for each other or for our children.
R. Lord, hear us.

That we may find our greatest joy in each other.
R. Lord, hear us.

That each of us may be quick to take our share of blame.
R. Lord, hear us.

That our disagreements may leave no trace of bitterness.
R. Lord, hear us.

That the sun may never go down on our anger.
R. Lord, hear us.

That we may create for our children a place of freedom, joy and peace.
R. Lord, hear us.

That we may be open and approachable, so that our children may find it easy to talk to us.
R. Lord, hear us.

That we may love and cherish all our children equally.
R. Lord, hear us.

Let us Pray
Lord, watch over us this night and always. Keep us safe from all harm and danger. As we grow older, may we find in each other ever greater strength. And may old age not find us lonely and bitter, but surrounded by the love of those we have brought into the world.

Then, Lord, when the time comes for one of us to die, may our love reach beyond death, and look forward to the happy day when we shall be forever one with you and with those we love. Amen.

7. Jesus falls the second time.

8. Jesus comforts the women of Jerusalem.

The Mysteries of the Rosary

The Joyful Mysteries
The Annunciation
The Visitation
The Birth of our Lord
The Presentation of our Lord
in the Temple
The finding of our Lord in the Temple

The Sorrowful Mysteries
The Agony of our Lord in the Garden
The Scourging at the Pillar
The Crowning with Thorns
The Carrying of the Cross
The Crucifixion and the Death
of our Lord

The Glorious Mysteries
The Resurrection of our Lord
The Ascension of our Lord into heaven
The Decent of the Holy Spirit
upon the apostles
The Assumption of our Blessed Mother
into heaven
The Coronation of our Blessed Mother
in heaven

Hail, holy Queen
Hail, holy Queen, mother of mercy,
hail our life, our sweetness and our
hope!
To you we cry, poor banished children
of Eve; to you we send up our sighs,
mourning and weeping in this vale of
tears. Turn then most gracious
advocate, your eyes of mercy towards
us; and after this our exile show to us
the blessed fruit of your womb, Jesus.
O clement, O loving, O sweet virgin
Mary. Pray for us, O holy Mother of
God. That we may be made worthy of
the promises of Christ.

Let us pray
O God, whose only begotten Son by
his life, death and resurrection has
purchased for us the rewards of eternal
life, grant, we beseech you, that
meditating on the mysteries of the
most holy Rosary of the Blessed Virgin
Mary, we may imitate what they
contain and obtain what they promise.
Through the same Christ, our Lord.
Amen.

30

9. Jesus falls the third time.

10. Jesus is stripped of his garments.

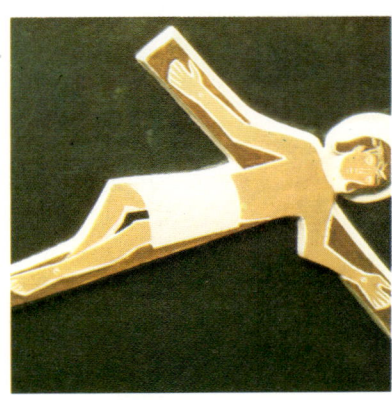

11. Jesus is nailed to the cross.

12. Jesus dies on the cross.

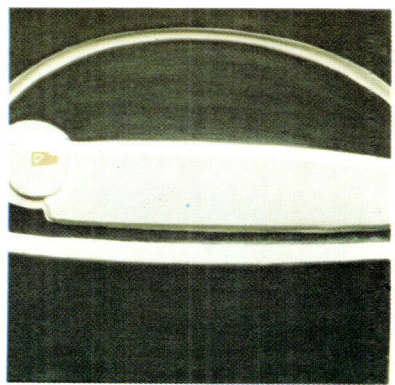

13. Jesus is taken down from the cross.

14. Jesus is laid in the tomb.

MAKING PLANS

It is good to plan our family prayers to ensure a certain amount of variety and freshness - and to make sure that they happen. Here is how one family planned their prayers. It may give you some ideas.

Sunday:
When did I feel loved by someone in this family today?
Chatting time, asking Mum and Dad "any questions". First Joyful Mystery. Night offering.

Monday:
When did I show/not show love today? Who most needs our prayers during this decade of the Rosary? Second Joyful Mystery.

Tuesday:
Who in the family hurt me recently? (Forgive). What happened today that I would like to thank God for in this decade? Third Joyful Mystery.

Wednesday:
What's my biggest worry/concern at the moment? What is the nicest thing about......(Joe)? Thank God for that. Fourth Joyful Mystery.

Thursday:
Whom did I hurt recently? (Ask forgiveness). What grace do I most want you all to pray for? (Hail Mary after each). Fifth Joyful Mystery.

Friday:
Mum or Dad tell/read the story of a saint and we pray with that saint for our special intentions. Hymn: Bind us together, Lord.

Saturday:
Dad tells the story of tomorrow's gospel in his own words and asks questions about it. We talk about why we are going to Mass and ask our Father to help us be attentive.